SONGS
RECORDED BY

DINAH WASHINGTON

VOLUME 8

MUSIC OF THE STARS
Rare Jazz and Popular Songs from The American Songbook

Produced by **John L. Haag**

Sales and Shipping:
PROFESSIONAL MUSIC INSTITUTE
4553 Rubio, Encino, CA 91436
sales@promusicbooks.com
www.promusicbooks.com

Suggestions and submissions for new products always welcome.

Ain't Nobody's Business If I Do

('tain't Nobody's Biz-ness If I Do)

Lyric and Music by
Porter Grainger and Everett Robbins

Verse

1. There ain't noth-in' I can do, nor noth-in' I can say,
2. Aft-ter all, the way to do is do just as you please,

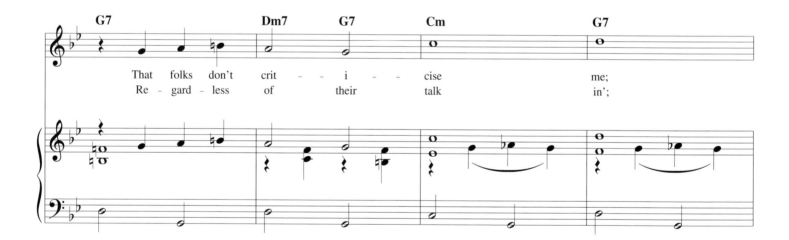

That folks don't crit - i - cise me;
Re - gard - less of their talk - in';

But I'm gon-na do just as I want to an-y-way,
O - ten times the ones that talk will get down on their knees,

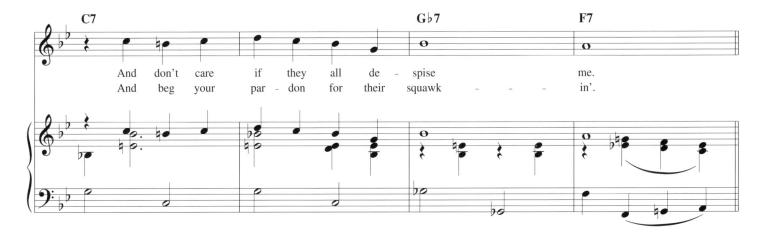

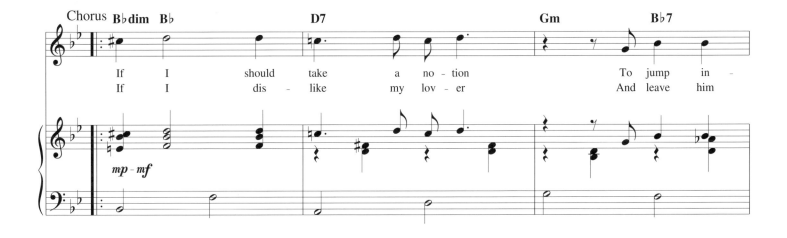

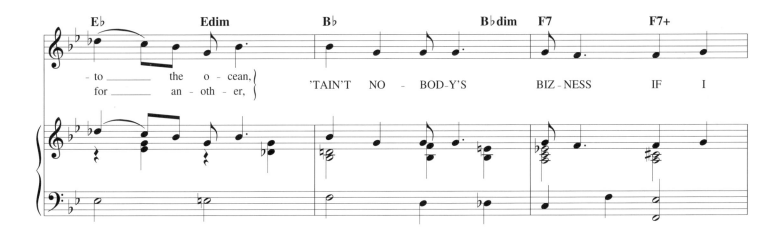

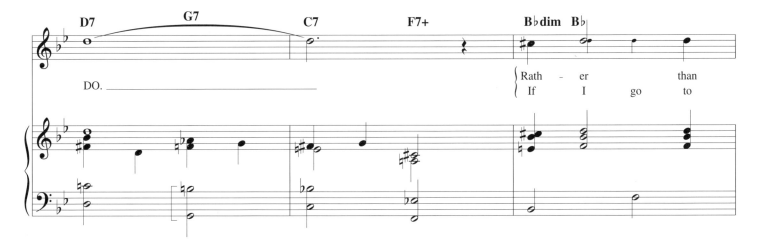

Ain't nobody's business if I do 2-4

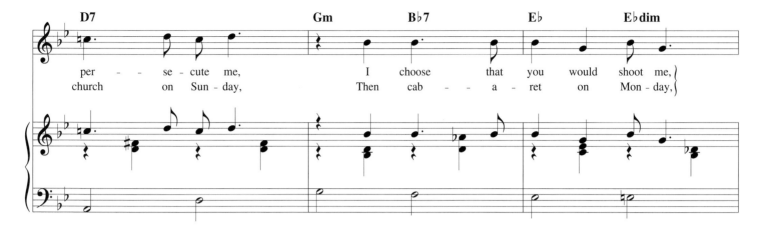

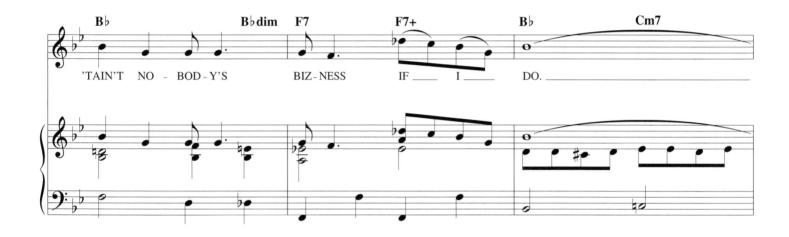

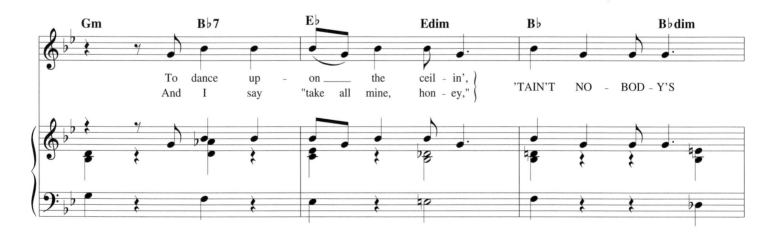

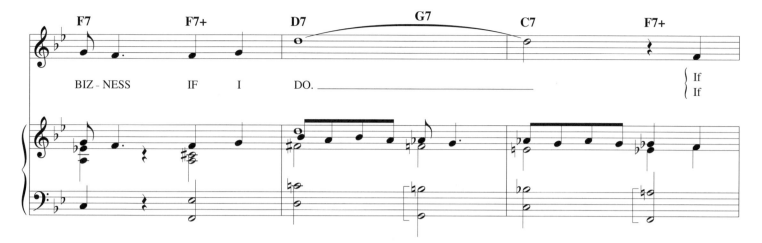

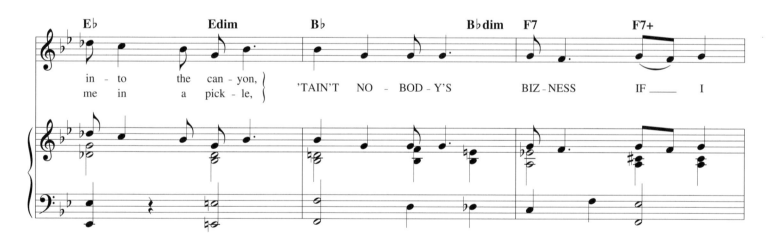

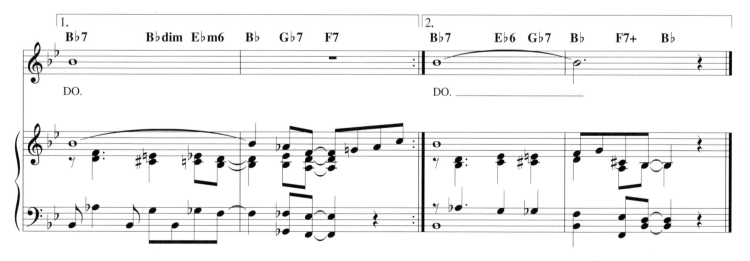

All Of Me

Lyric and Music by
Seymour Simons and Gerald Marks

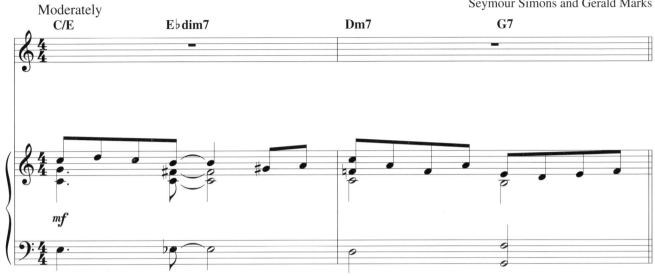

You took my kiss - es and you took my love, ___ You taught me how to

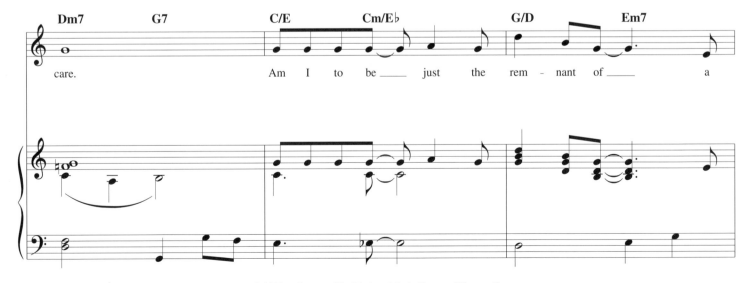

care. Am I to be ___ just the rem - nant of ___ a

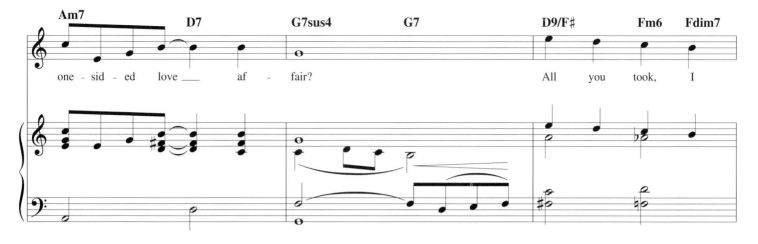

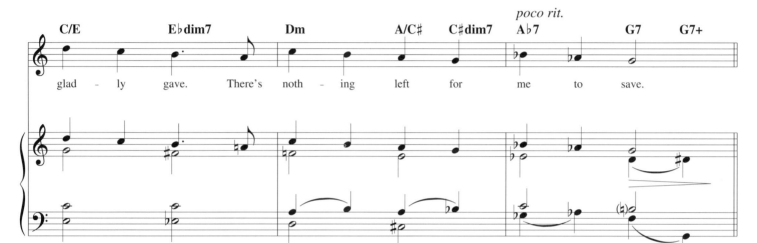

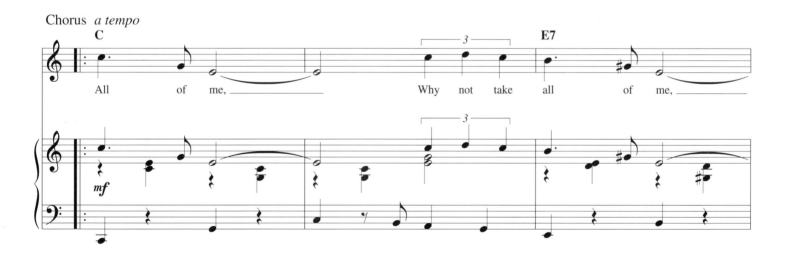

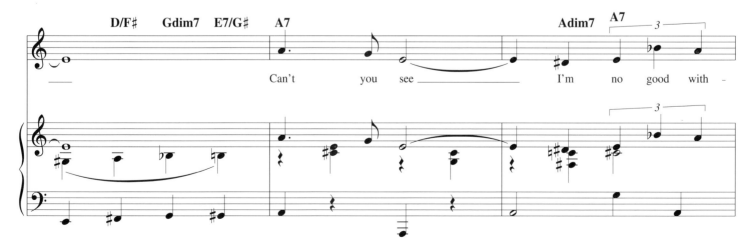

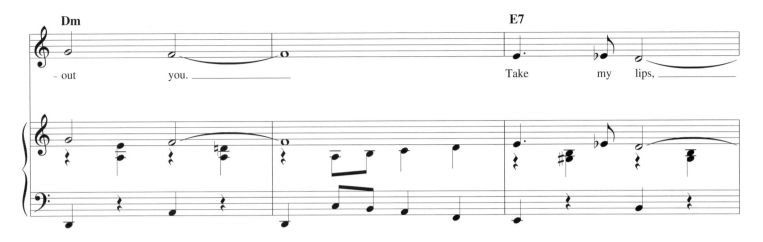

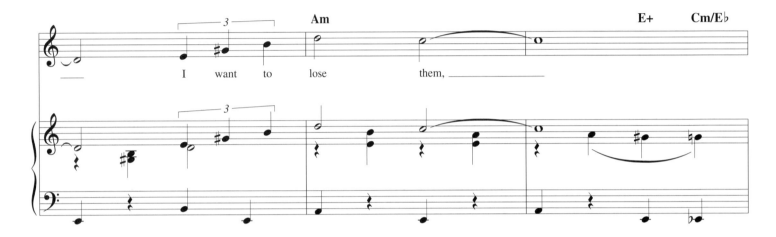

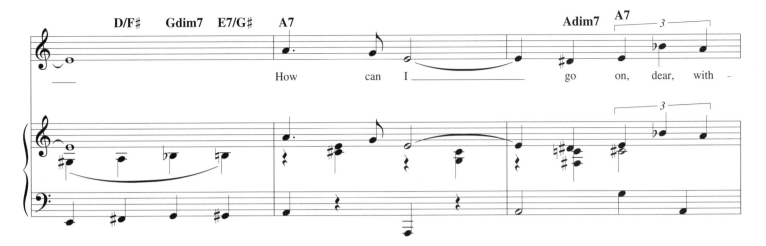

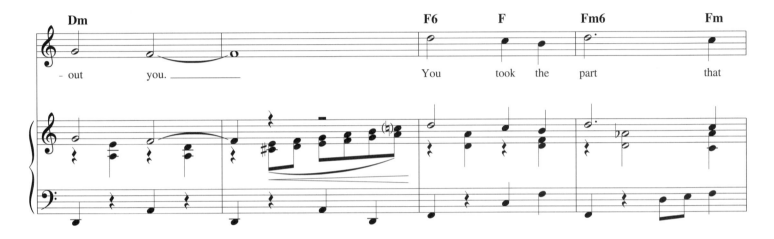

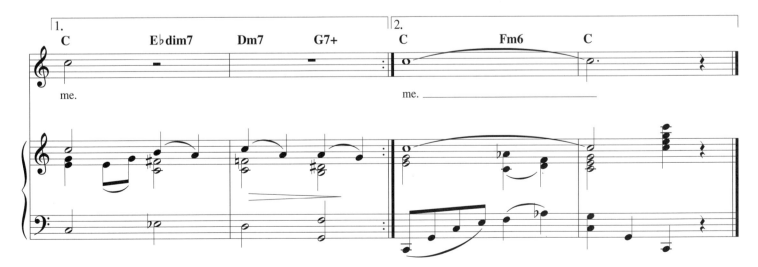

All of me 4-4

Baby, Won't You Please Come Home?

Lyric and Music by
Charles Warfield and Clarence Williams

Ba - by, won't you please come home, 'Cause your mam-ma's all a - lone

I have tried in vain, nev - er no more to call, your name

When you left you broke my heart. _____ Be-

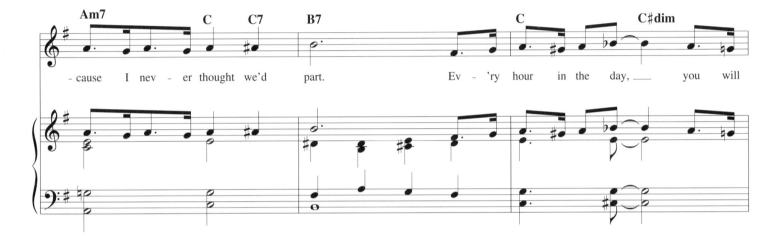

-cause I nev-er thought we'd part. Ev-'ry hour in the day, ___ you will

hear me say, ___ Ba-by won't you please come home

home Dad-dy needs mam-ma, Ba-by won't you please come home. _____

Baby, won't you please come home? 2-2

The Birth Of The Blues

Lyric by B. G. DeSylva and Lew Brown
Music by Ray Henderson

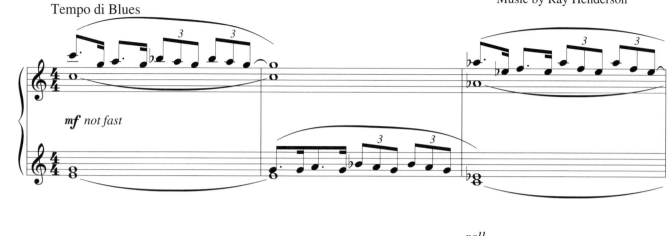

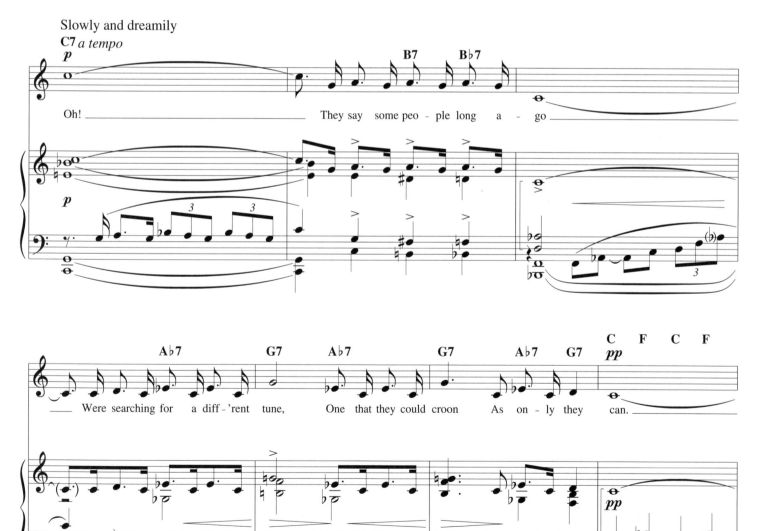

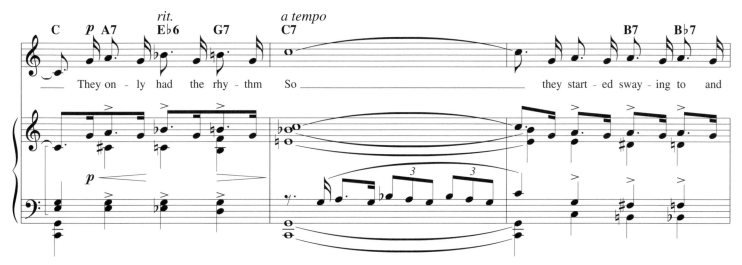

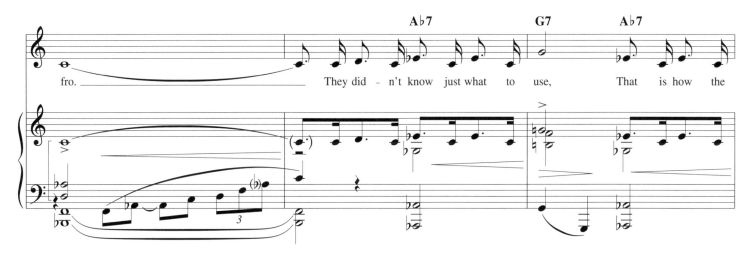

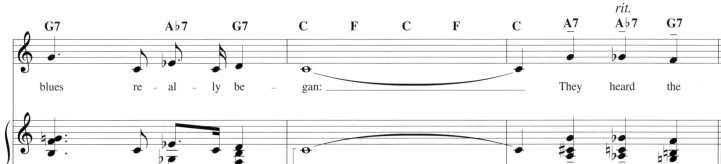

The birth of the blues 2-4

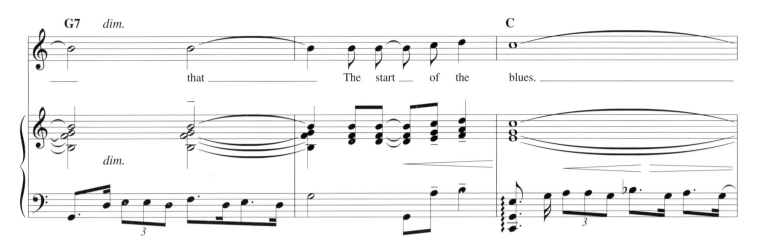

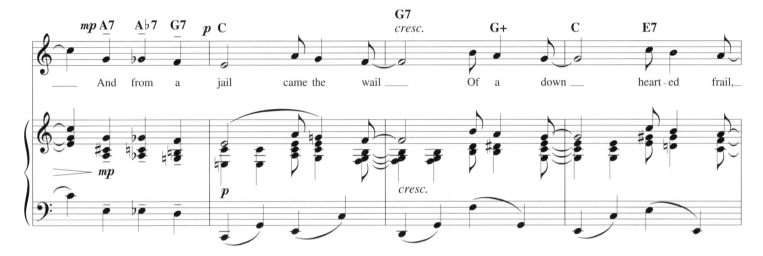

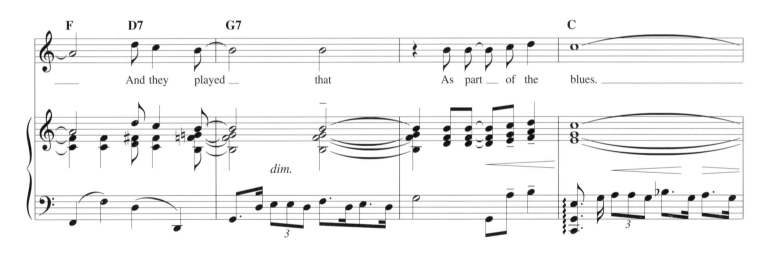

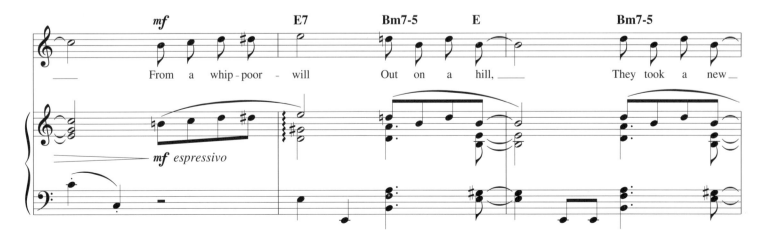

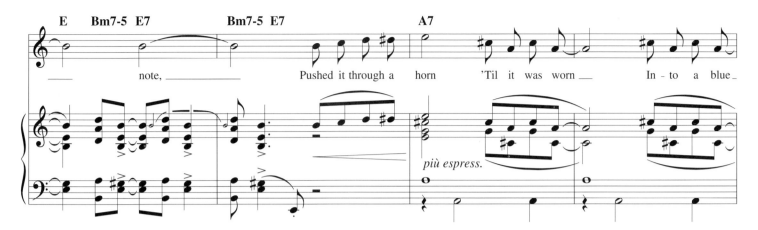

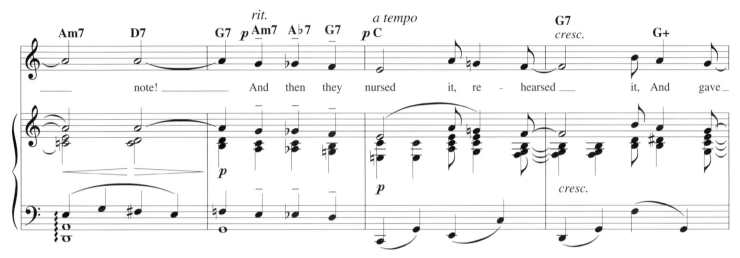

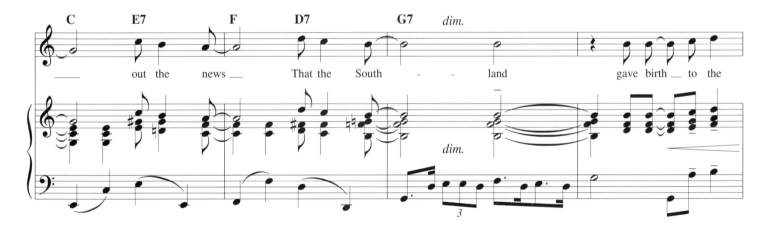

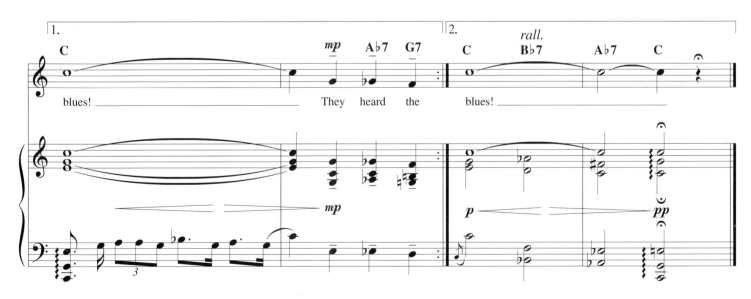

The birth of the blues 4-4

Blue Gardenia

Lyric and Music by
Bob Russell and Lester Lee

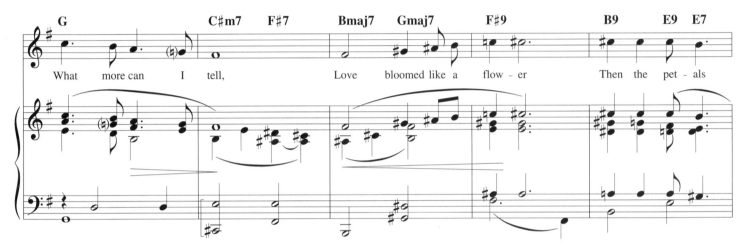

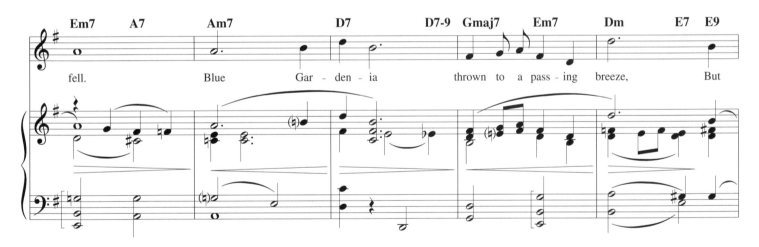

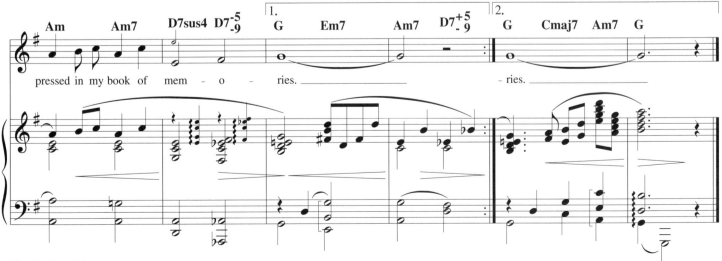

Blue Gardenia 2-2

Destination Moon

Lyric by Roy Alfred
Music by Marvin Fisher

Medium bounce

Come and take a trip __ in my rock - et ship, __ We'll have a love - ly af - ter -

- noon, __ Kiss the world good - bye and a - way we fly __ *(Shhhh)* __ des - ti - na - tion

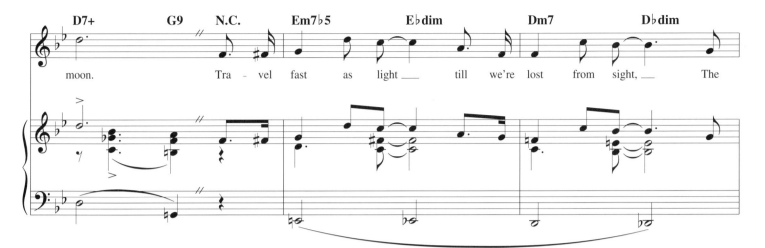

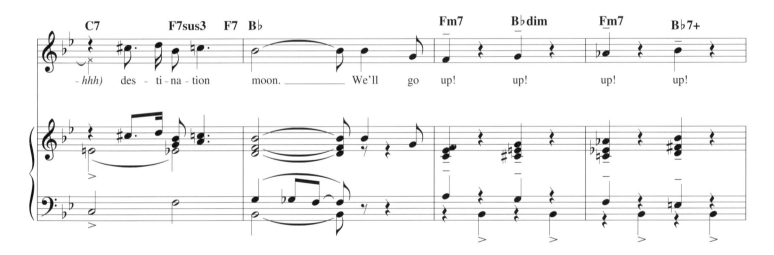

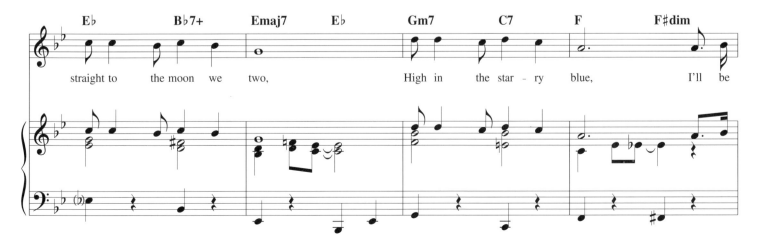

Destination moon 2-3

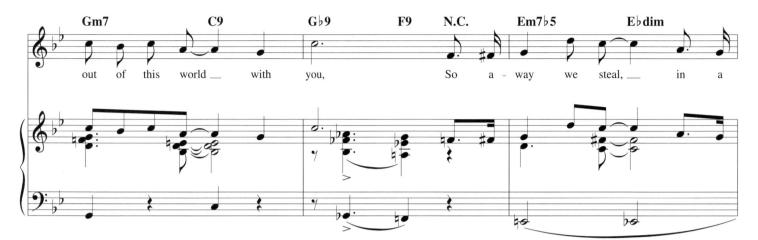

out of this world __ with you, So a-way we steal, __ in a

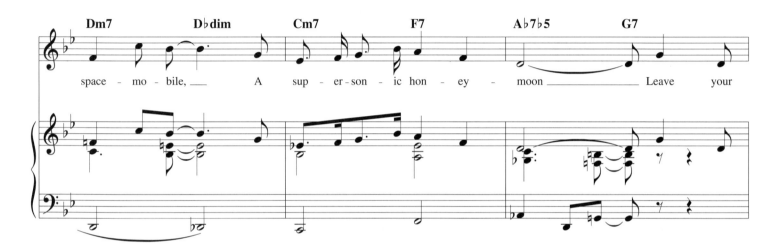

space - mo - bile, __ A sup - er-son - ic hon - ey - moon _____ Leave your

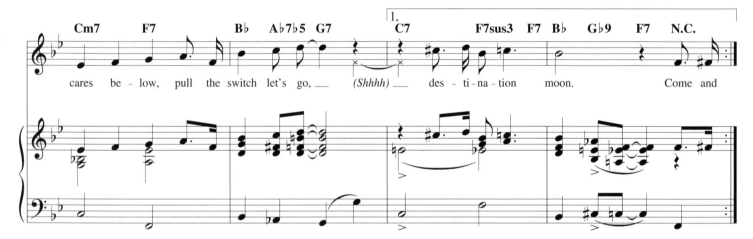

cares be - low, pull the switch let's go, __ (Shhhh) __ des - ti - na - tion moon. Come and

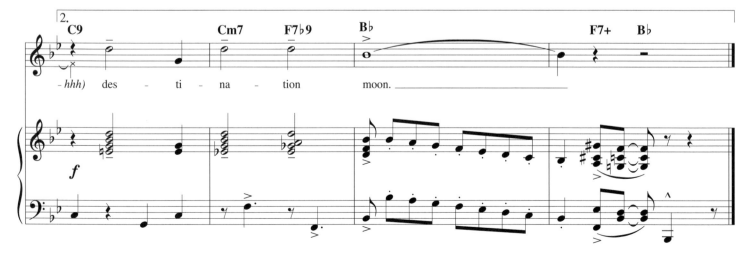

-hhh) des - ti - na - tion moon. _____

Destination moon 3-3

After You've Gone

Lyric and Music by
Henry Creamer and Turner Layton

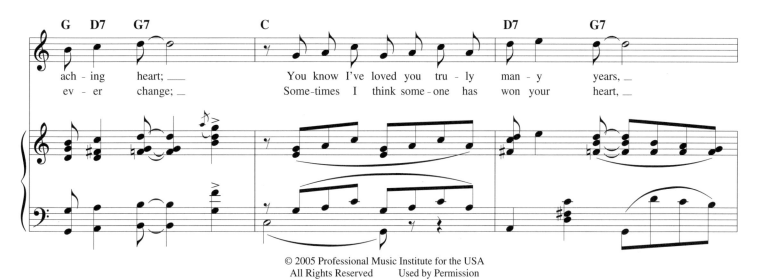

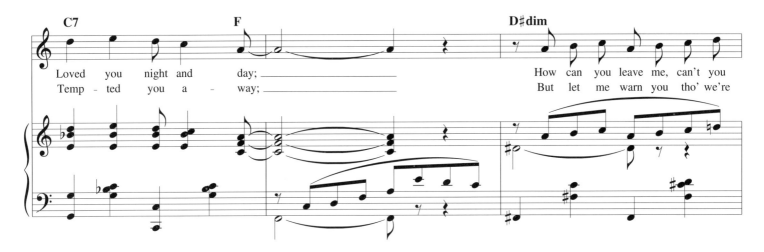

Loved you night and day;_____ How can you leave me, can't you
Temp - ted you a - way;_____ But let me warn you tho' we're

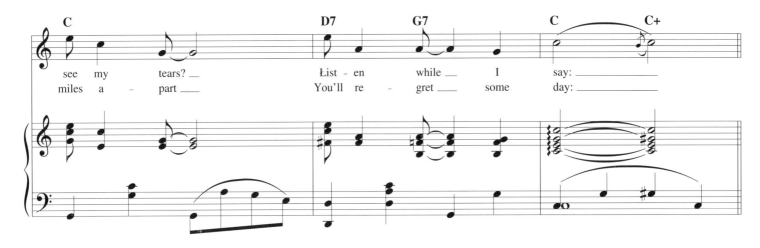

see my tears?__ List - en while __ I say:_____
miles a - part __ You'll re - gret __ some day:_____

Chorus

Af - ter you've gone, __ and left me cry-ing; Af - ter you've gone, __ There's no de - ny-ing;
Af - ter I'm gone, __ af - ter we break up; Af - ter I'm gone, __ You're gonna wake up;

you'll feel blue, __ You'll feel sad, __ You'll miss the dear - est pal you've
you will find, __ You were blind, __ To let some - bod - y come and

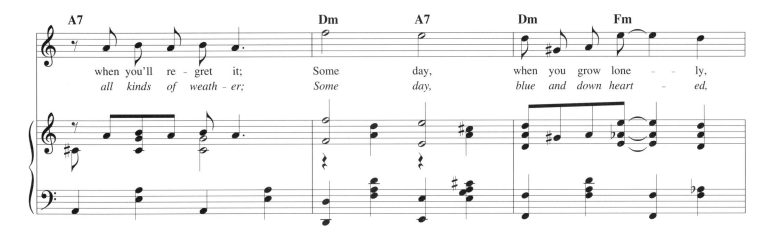

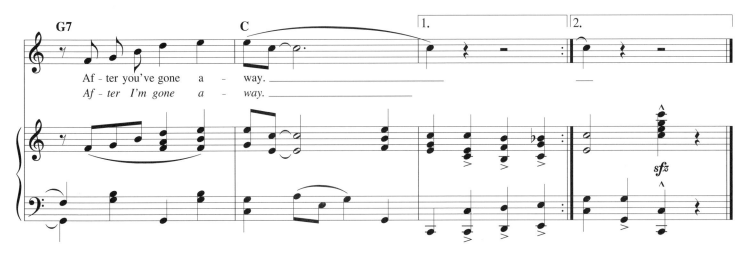

After you've gone 3-3

Do Nothin' Till You Hear From Me

Lyric by Bob Russell
Music by Duke Ellington

Do nothin' till you hear from me 2-3

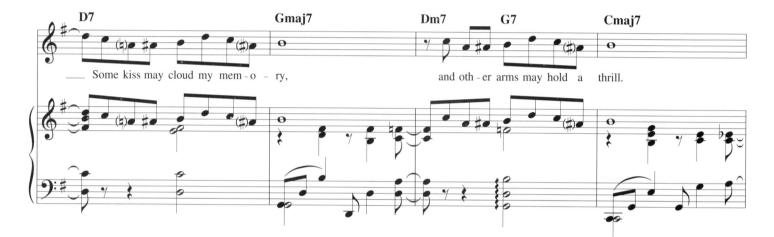

For All We Know

Lyric by Haven Gillespie
Music by J. Fred Coots

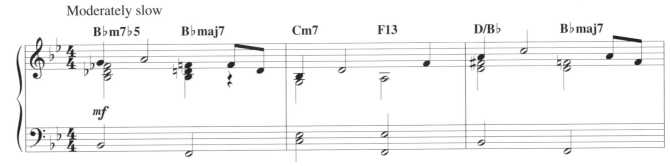

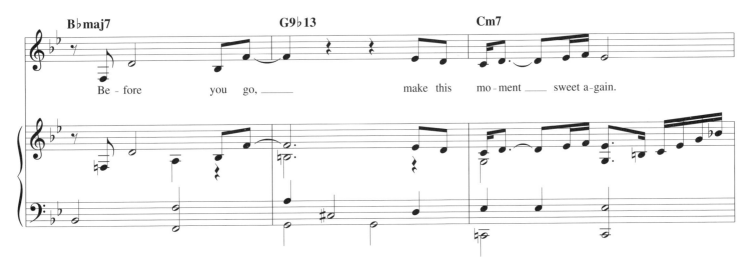

28

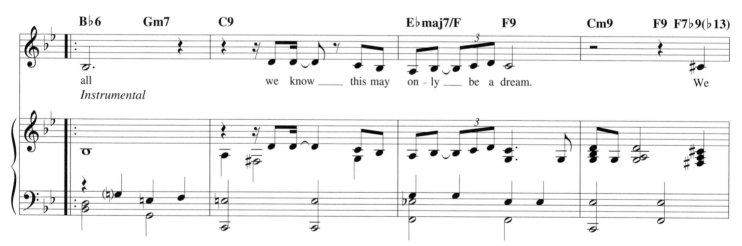

For all we know 2-3

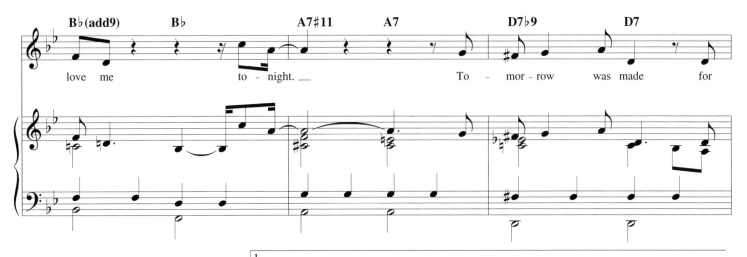

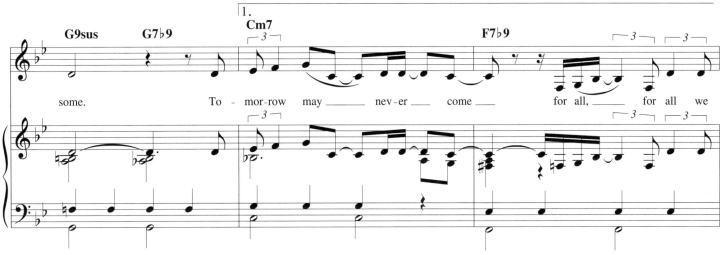

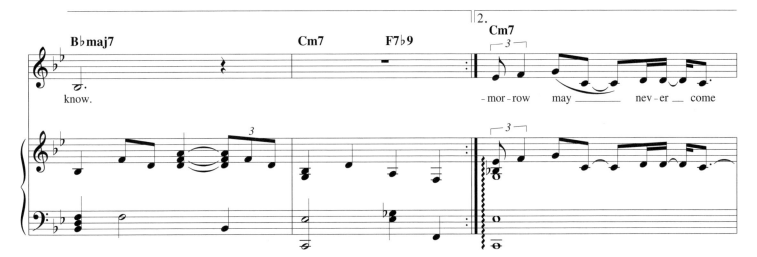

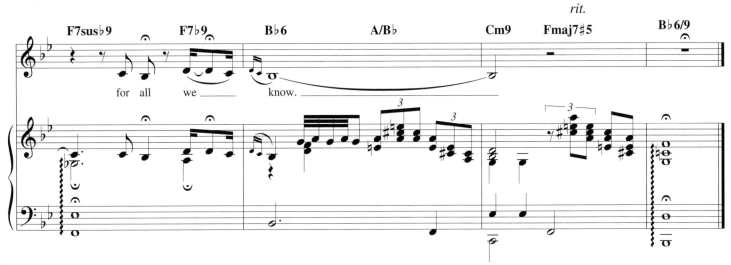

For all we know 3-3

There Goes My Heart

Lyric by Benny Davis
Music by Abner Silver

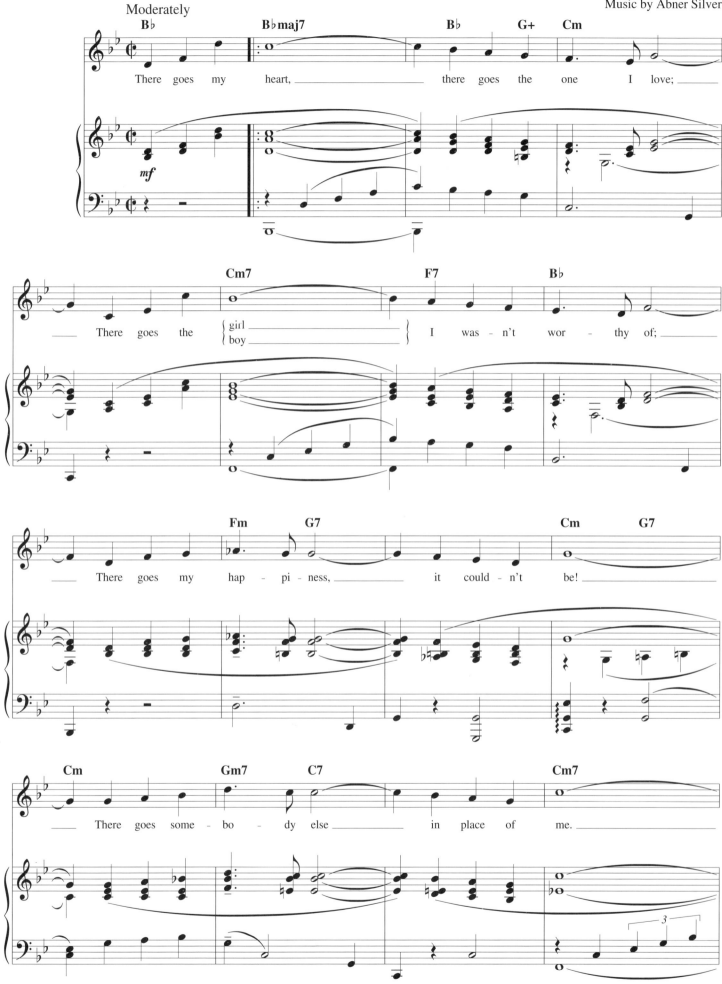

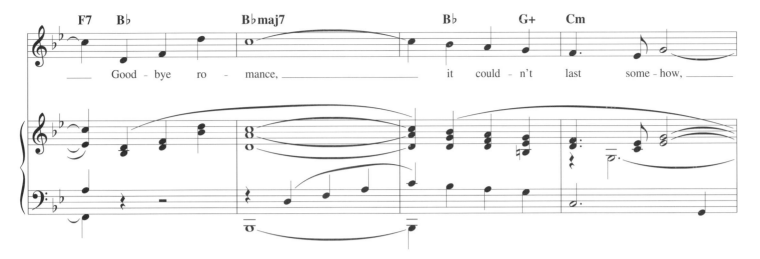

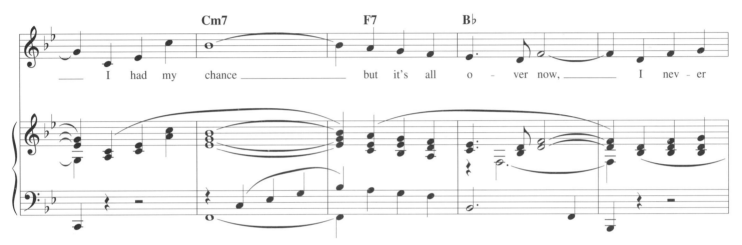

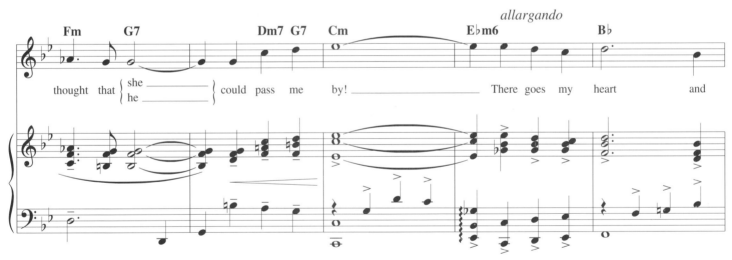

I Didn't Know About You

Lyric by Bob Russell
Music by Duke Ellington

I ran a - round with my

own lit - tle crowd. The u – su – al laughs; not of - ten, but loud. And in the

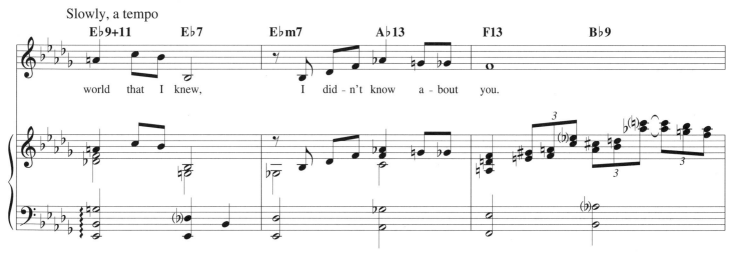

Slowly, a tempo

world that I knew, I did-n't know a - bout you.

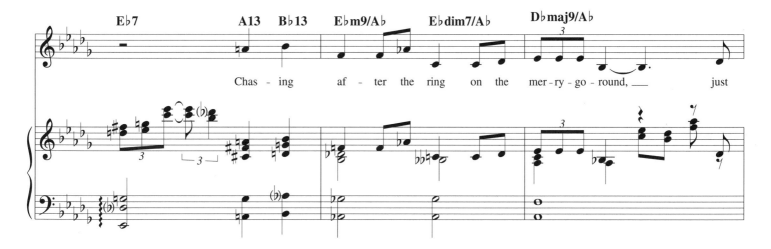

Chas - ing af - ter the ring on the mer-ry-go-round, ___ just

tak - ing my fun ___ where it could be found. ___ And yet what else could I do?

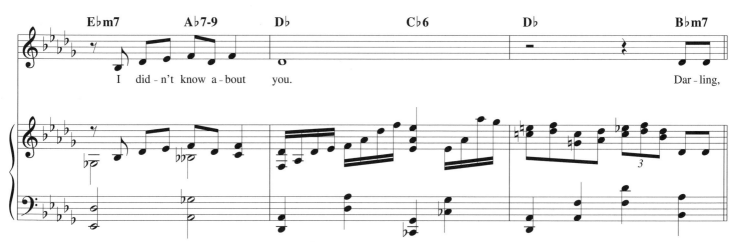

I did - n't know a-bout you. Dar - ling,

I didn't know about you 2-4

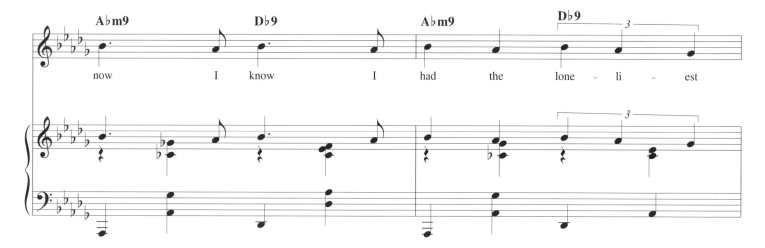

now   I   know   I   had   the   lone - li - est

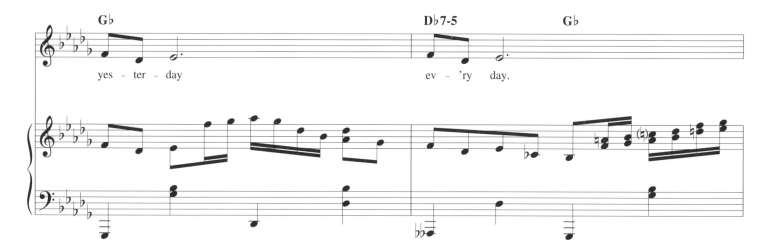

yes - ter - day   ev - 'ry   day.

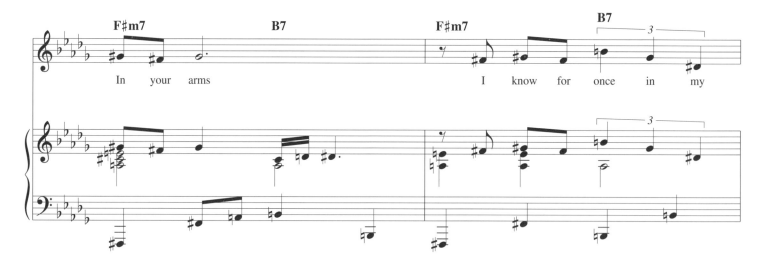

In   your   arms   I   know   for   once   in   my

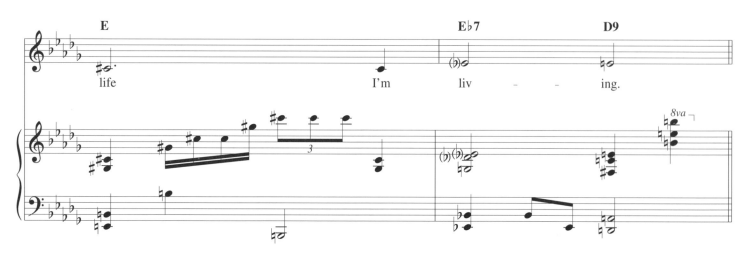

life   I'm   liv - - ing.

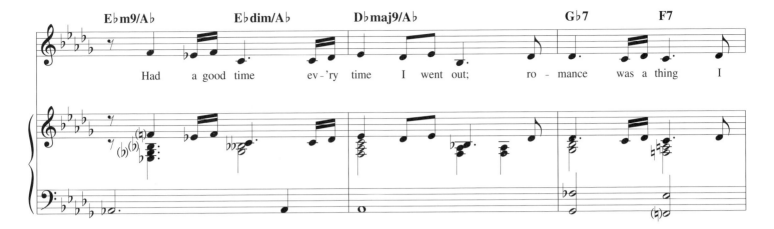

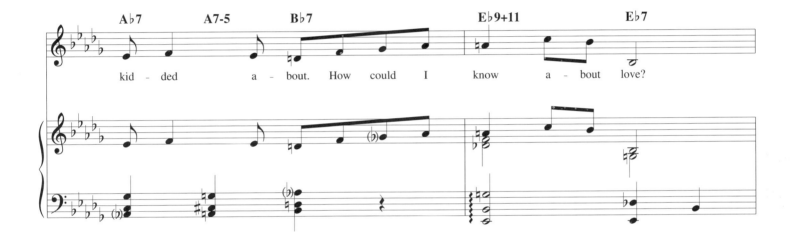

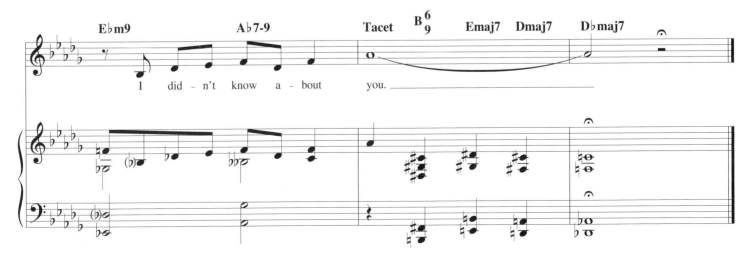

Good Morning Heartache

Lyric and Music by
Ervin Drake, Irene Higginbotham and Dan Fisher

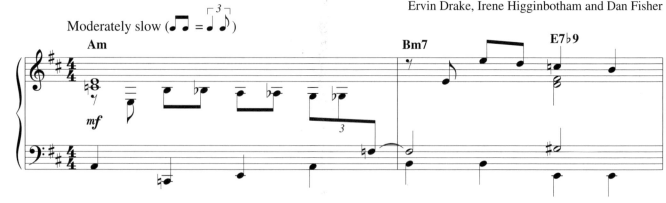

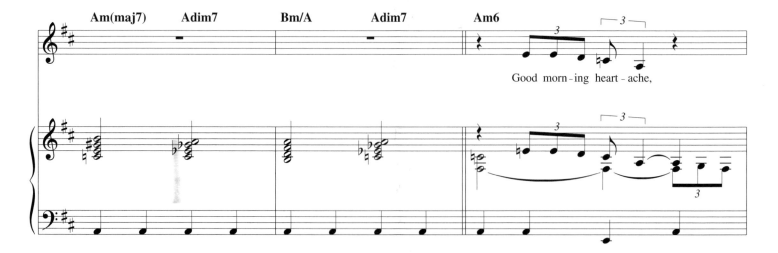

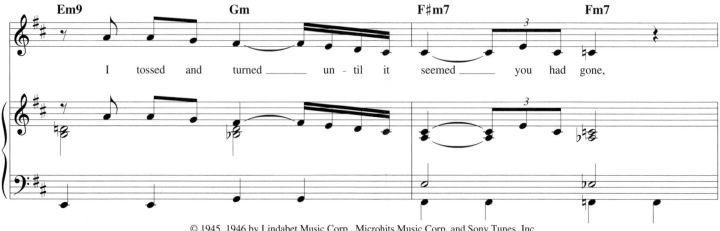

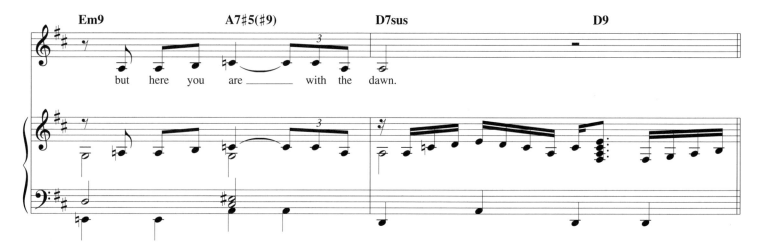

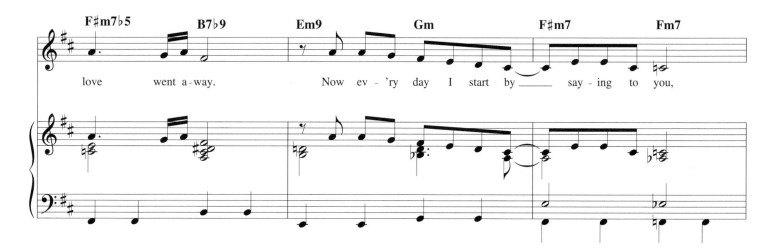

Good morning heartache 2-4

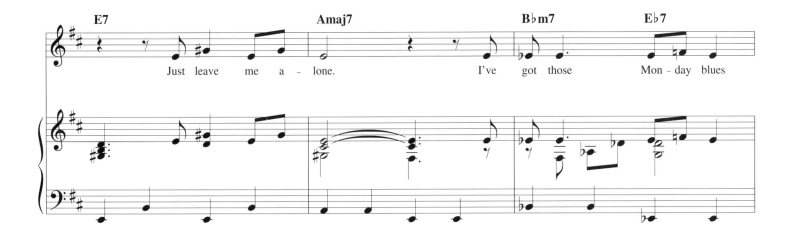

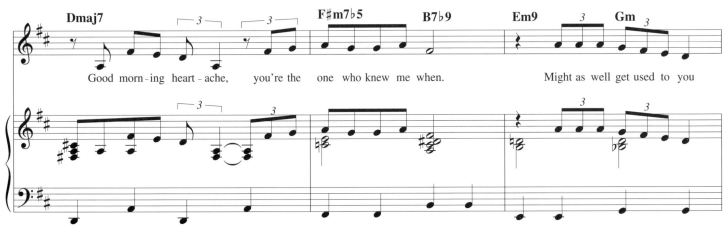

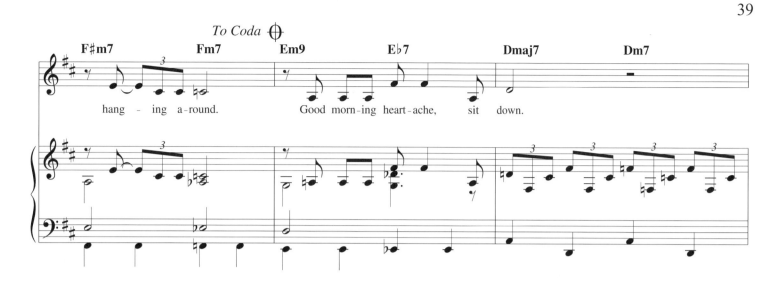

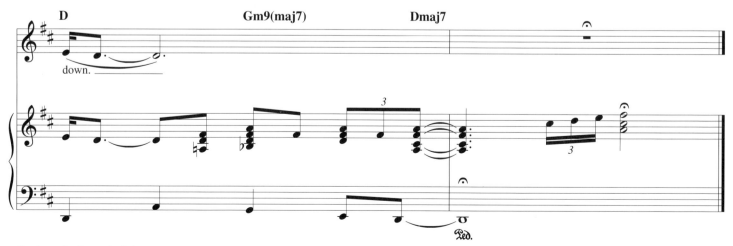

Good morning heartache 4-4

I Won't Cry Anymore

Lyric by Fred Wise
Music by Al Frisch

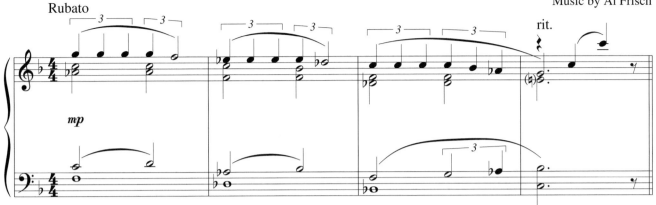

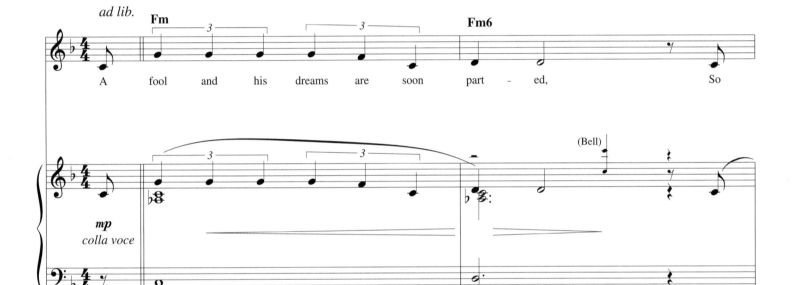

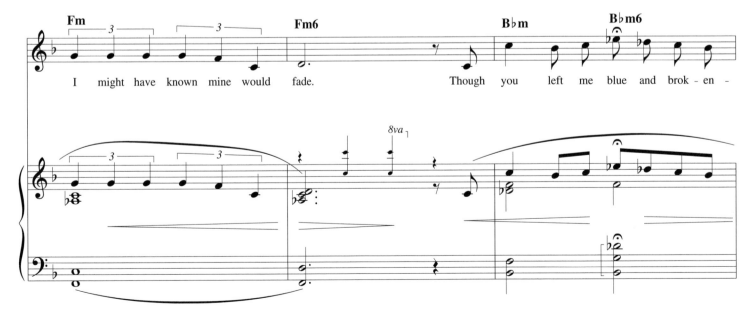

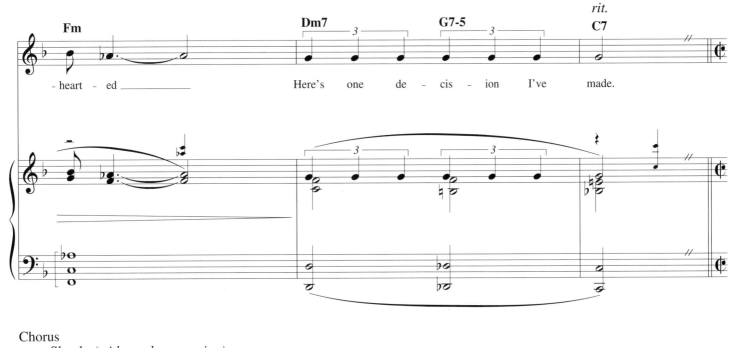

Fm   Dm7   G7-5   *rit.*   C7

-heart - ed _____ Here's one de - ci - sion I've made.

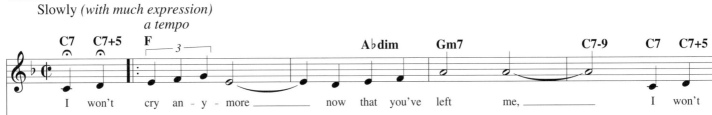

Chorus
Slowly *(with much expression)*
     a tempo

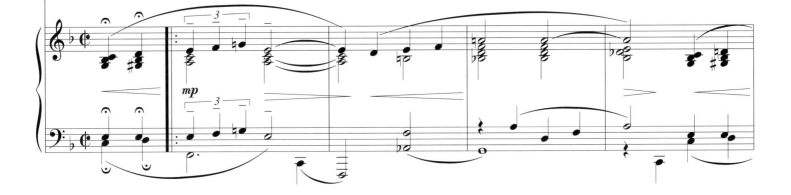

C7   C7+5   F   A♭dim   Gm7   C7-9   C7   C7+5

I won't cry an - y - more _____ now that you've left me, _____ I won't

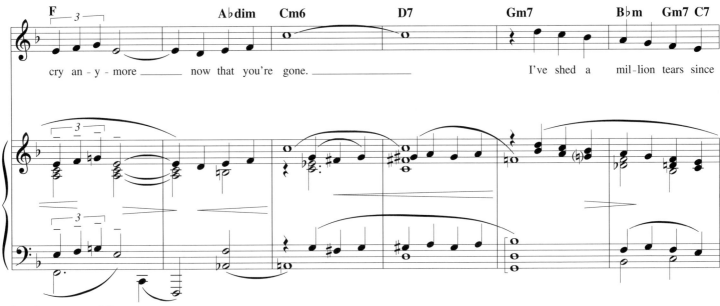

F   A♭dim   Cm6   D7   Gm7   B♭m   Gm7 C7

cry an - y - more _____ now that you're gone. _____ I've shed a mil - lion tears since

I won't cry anymore 2-3

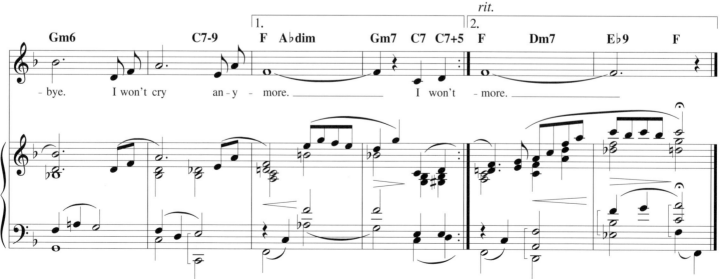

More Than You Know

Lyric by Billy Rose and Edward Eliscu
Music by Vincent Youmans

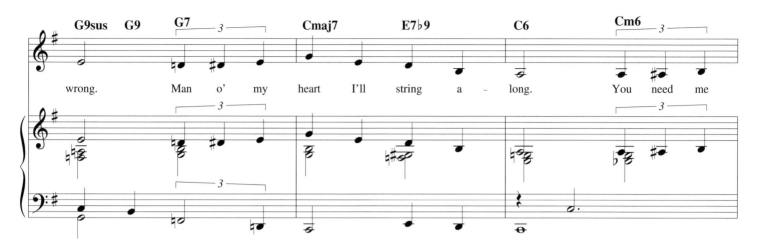

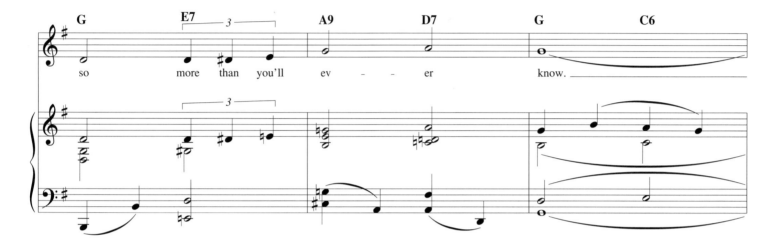

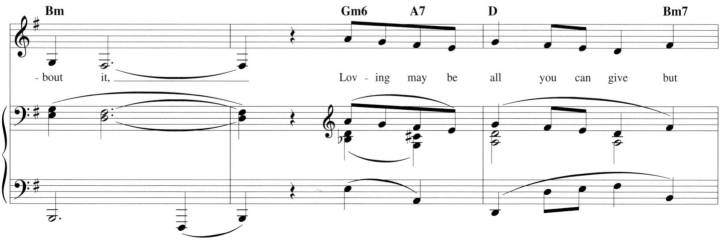

More than you know 2-3

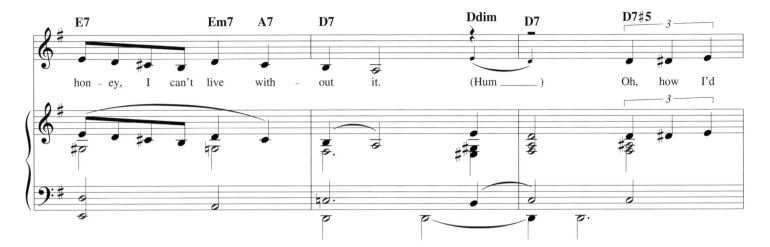

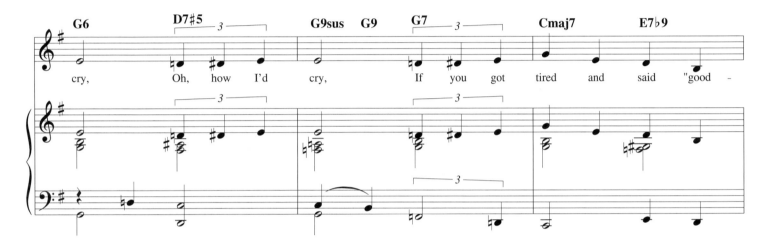

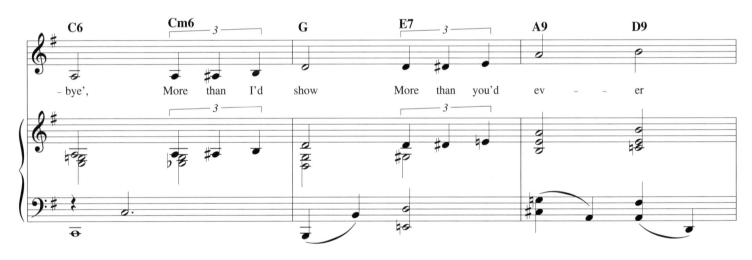

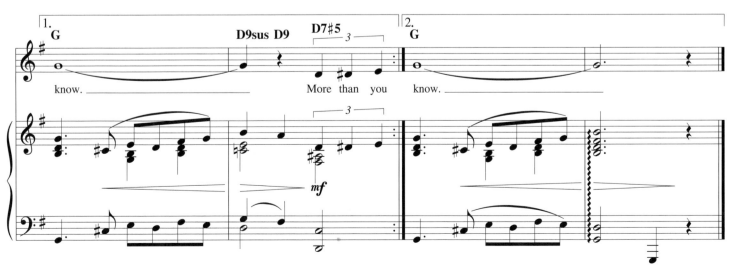

There'll Be Some Changes Made

Lyric by Billy Higgins
Music by Benton Overstreet

They say   don't change the old
They say   the   old - time things

for   the   new, ____
are   the   best, ____

But I've   found out   that this   will,
That   may   be ver - y   good for

There'll be some changes made 2-4

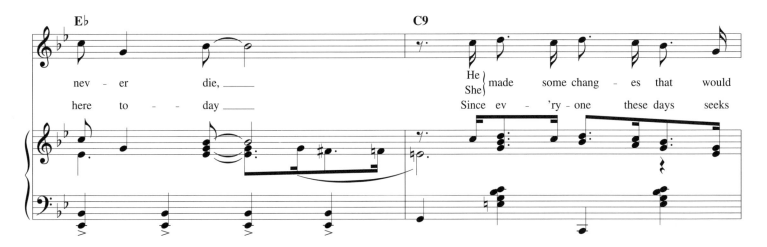

There'll be some changes made 3-4

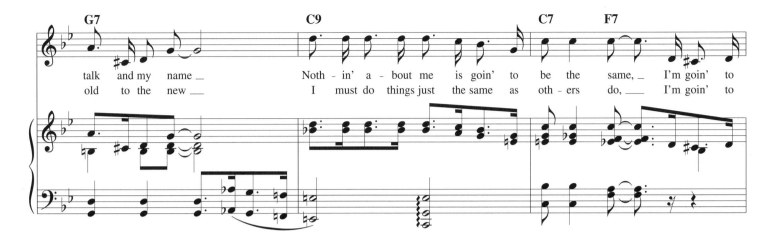

talk and my name __ Noth-in' a-bout me is goin' to be the same, __ I'm goin' to
old to the new __ I must do things just the same as oth-ers do, __ I'm goin' to

change my way of liv - in' if that ain't e - nough, __ Then I'll change the way that I
change my long, tall {Mam - ma / Dad - dy} for a lit-tle short Fat, __ Goin' to change the num - ber where

Strut my stuff, __ 'cause no-bod - y wants __ you when you're old and gray __ There'll be some chang-es
I live at. __ I must have some lov - in' or I'll fade a - way, __ There'll be some chang-es

made to - day __ There'll be some chang - es made. For there's a made.
made to - day __ There'll be some chang - es made. For there's a made.

They Didn't Believe Me

Lyric by Herbert Reynolds
Music by Jerome Kern

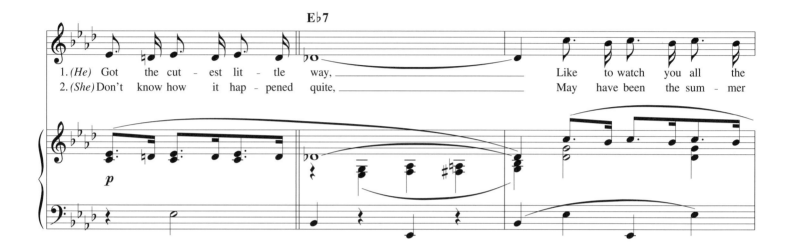

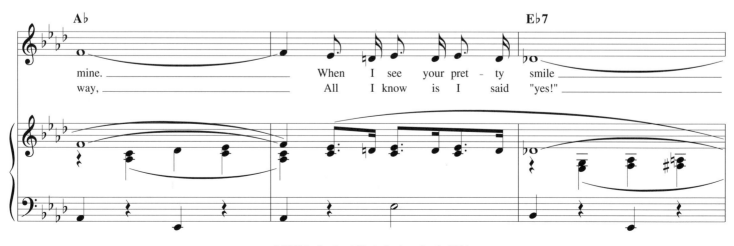

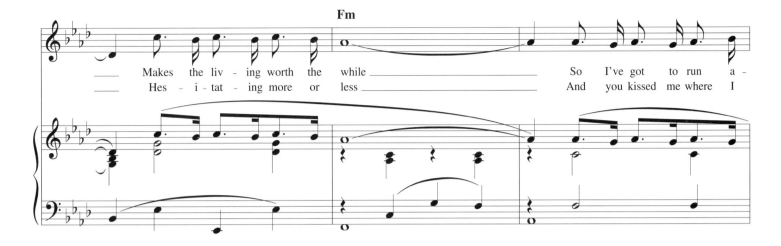

Makes the liv - ing worth the while _____ So I've got to run a -
Hes - i - tat - ing more or less _____ And you kissed me where I

- round _____ Tell - ing peo - ple what I've found. _____
stood _____ Just like an - y fel - low would. _____

Refrain

(He) And when I told them _____ How beau - ti - ful you are _____
(She) And when I told them _____ How won - der - ful you are _____

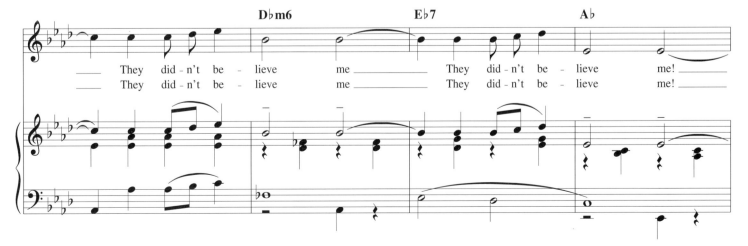

_____ They did - n't be - lieve me _____ They did - n't be - lieve me!
_____ They did - n't be - lieve me _____ They did - n't be - lieve me!

52

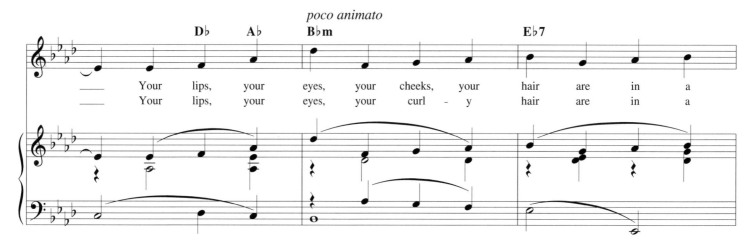

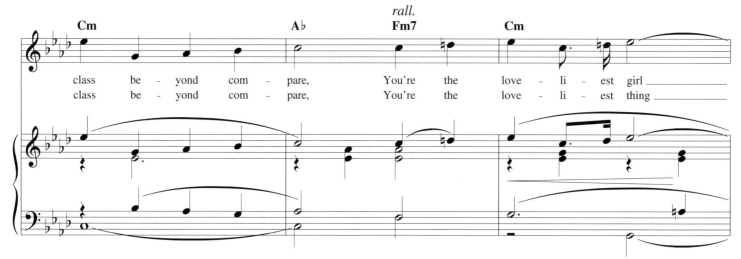

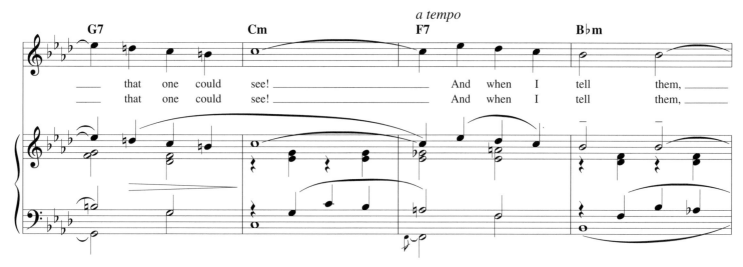

They didn't believe me 3-4

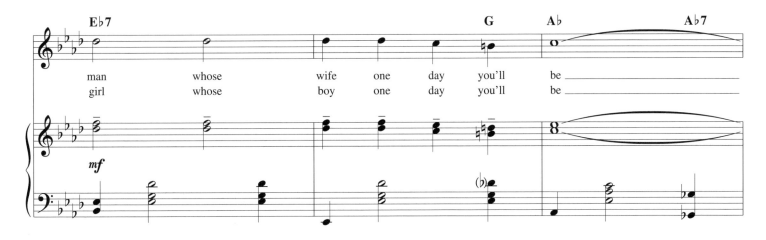

man   whose   wife   one   day   you'll   be _____
girl   whose   boy   one   day   you'll   be _____

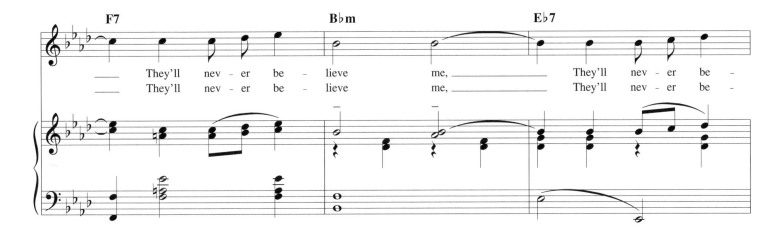

_____ They'll nev - er be - lieve   me, _____ They'll nev - er be -
_____ They'll nev - er be - lieve   me, _____ They'll nev - er be -

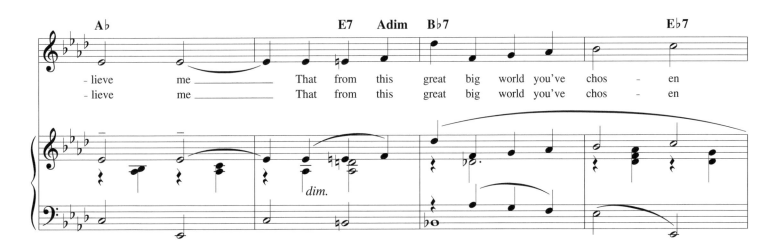

- lieve   me _____ That from this great big world you've chos - en
- lieve   me _____ That from this great big world you've chos - en

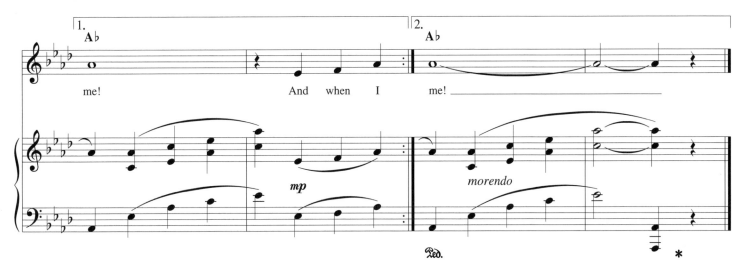

me!   And when I   me! _____

They didn't believe me 4-4

Without A Song

Lyric by Billy Rose and Edward Eliscu
Music by Vincent Youmans

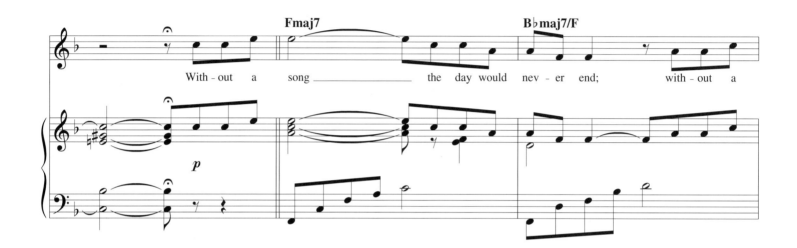

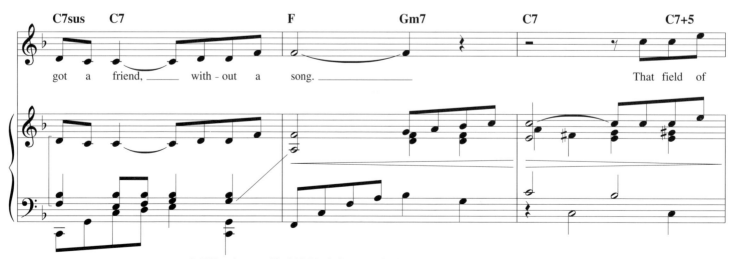

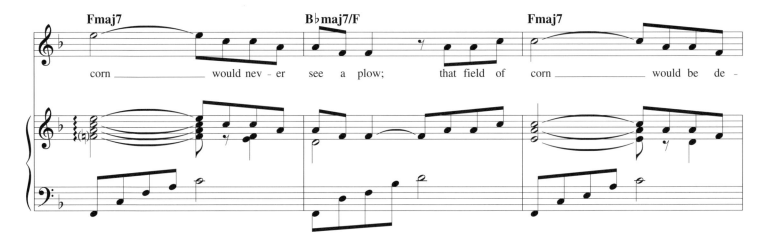

corn _____ would nev - er see a plow; that field of corn _____ would be de -

- sert - ed now; a man is born, _____ but he's no good no - how, _____ with out a

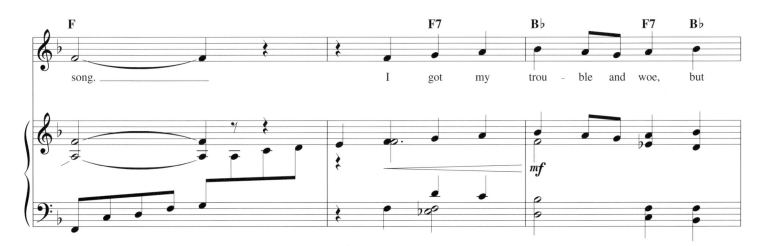

song. _____ I got my trou - ble and woe, but

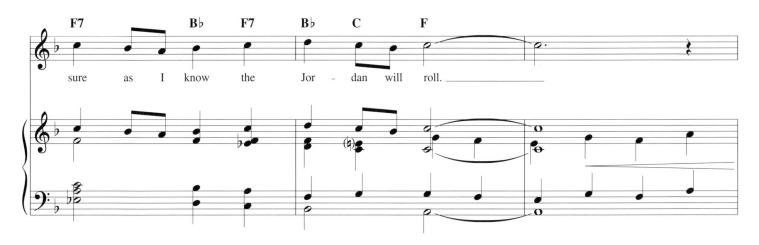

sure as I know the Jor - dan will roll. _____

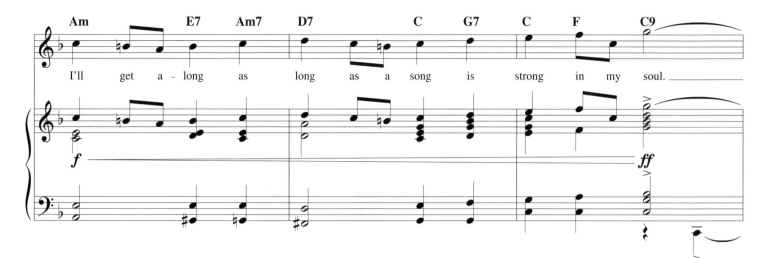

I'll get a-long as long as a song is strong in my soul. _____

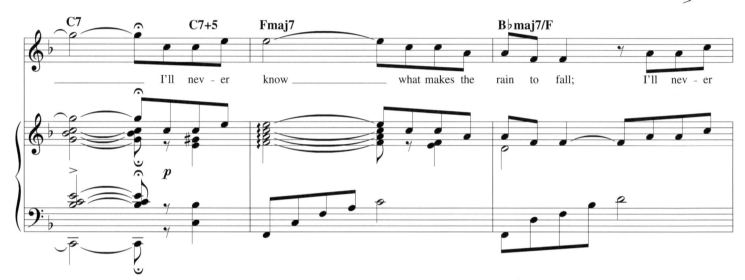

_____ I'll nev-er know _____ what makes the rain to fall; I'll nev-er

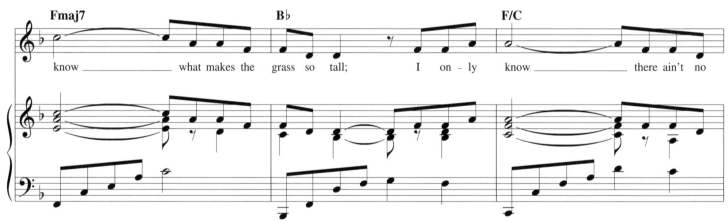

know _____ what makes the grass so tall; I on-ly know _____ there ain't no

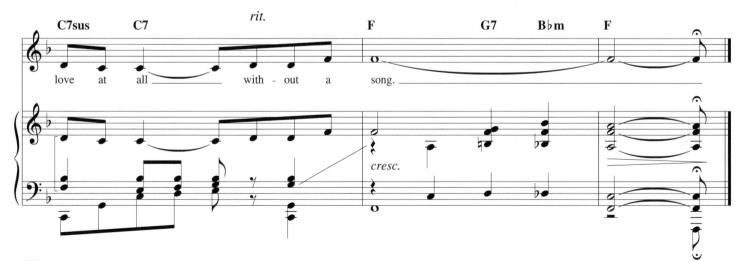

love at all _____ with-out a song. _____

Teach Me Tonight

Lyric by Sammy Cahn
Music by Gene DePaul

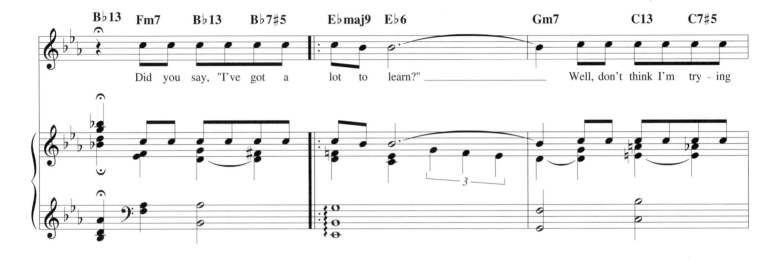

Did you say, "I've got a lot to learn?" _____ Well, don't think I'm try - ing

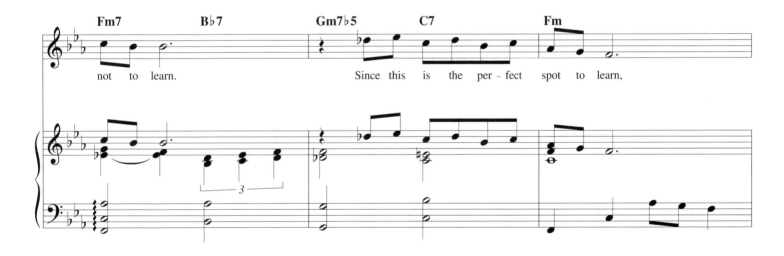

not to learn. Since this is the per - fect spot to learn, teach me to - night.

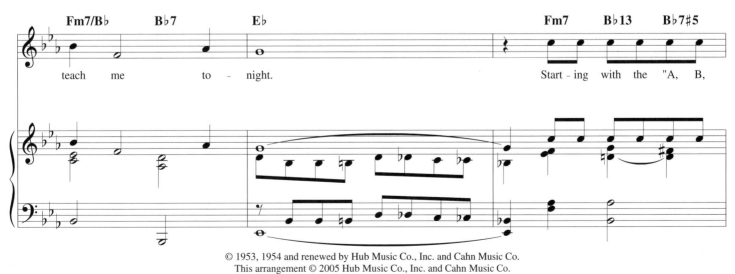

teach me to - night. Start - ing with the "A, B,

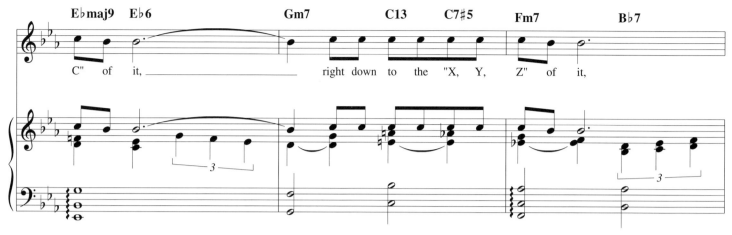

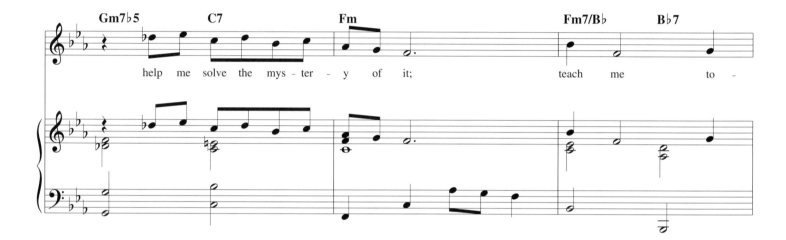

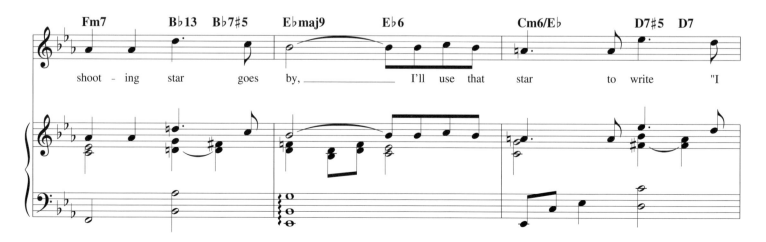

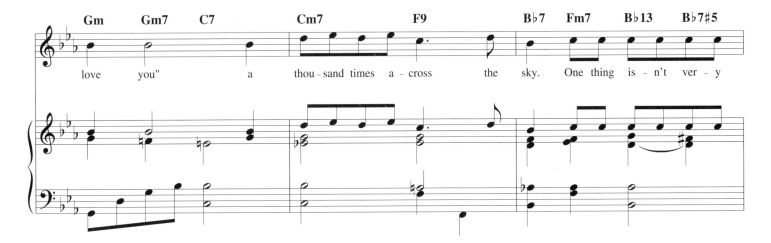

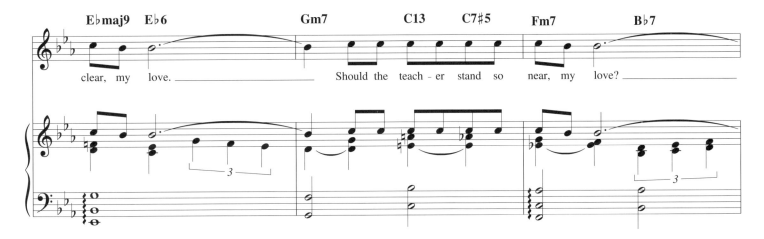

Teach me tonight 3-3

You Go To My Head

Lyric by Haven Gillespie
Music by J. Fred Coots

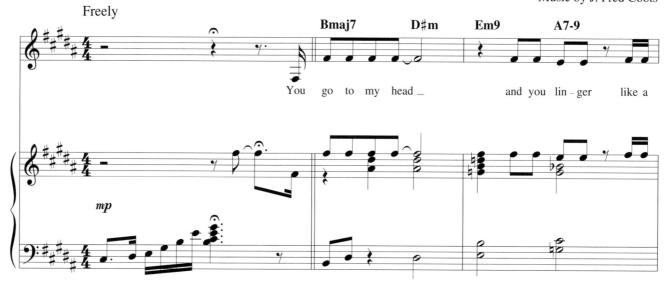

go to my head ___ like a sip of spar-kling bur-gun-dy brew, ___

and I find the ver - y men-tion of you ___ like the kick-er in a

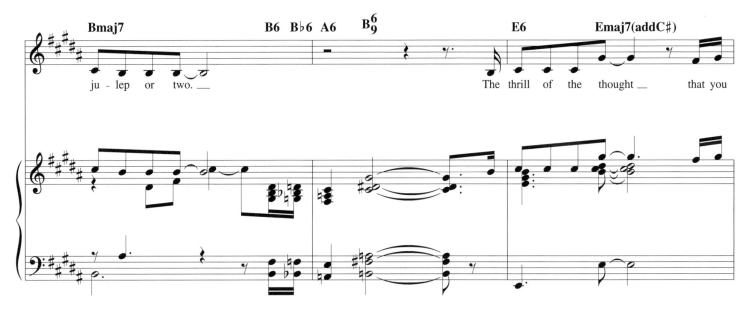

ju - lep or two. ___ The thrill of the thought ___ that you

62

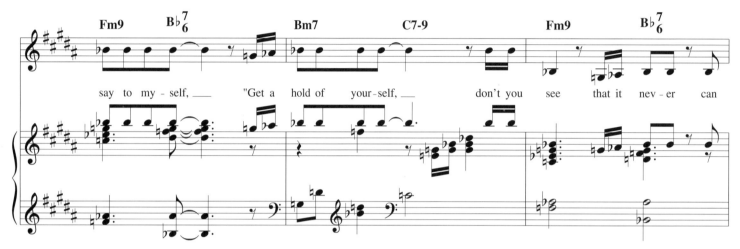

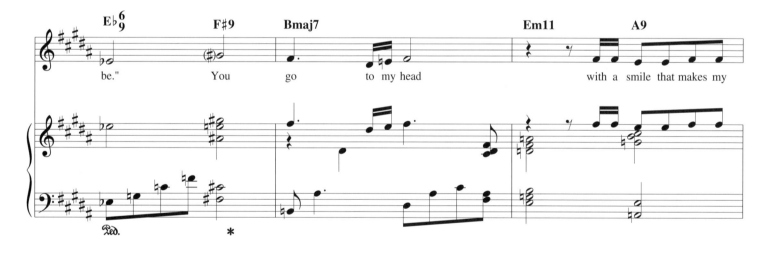

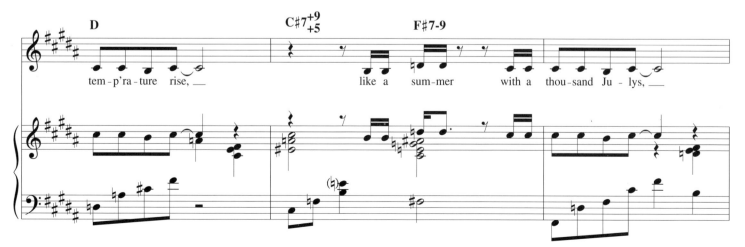

You go to my head 3-4

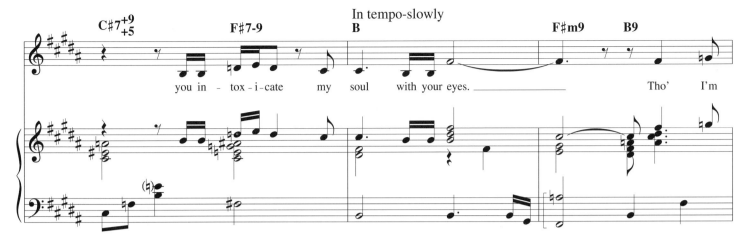

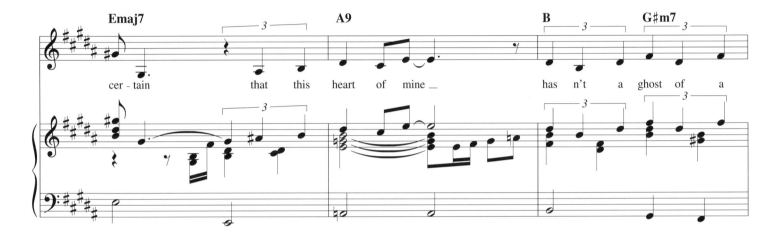

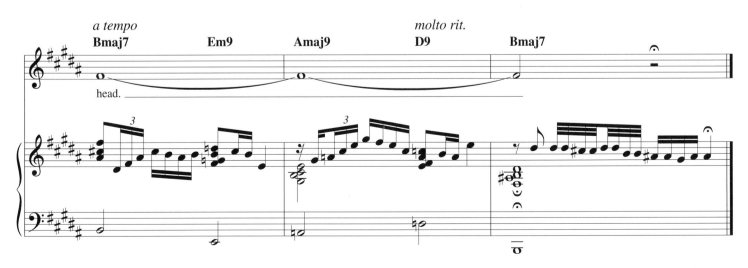

Selected Discography

After You've Gone
Dinah Washington "Dinah Sings Bessie Smith"
Anita O'Day "My Ship"
Judy Garland "Miss Show Business/Judy"

Ain't Nobody's Business If I Do
Dinah Washington "Queen Of The Blues"
Billie Holiday "Complete Decca Recordings"
Bessie Smith "Greatest Hits"

All Of Me
Dinah Washington "The Definitive Dinah Washington"
Susannah McCorkle "Dream"
Nnenna Freelon "Blueprint Of A Lady"

Baby, Won't You Please Come Home?
Dinah Washington "Best Of Dinah-The Roulette Years"
Julie London "Best Of Julie London"
Ella Fitzgerald "Ella In Hollywood"

The Birth Of The Blues
Dinah Washington "Dinah!"
Keely Smith "Wild, Cool & Swinging"
Niki Harris "Live In Switzerland"

Blue Gardenia
Dinah Washington "The Definitive Dinah Washington"
Diane Schuur "The Best Of Diane Schuur"
Etta James "Blue Gardenia"

Destination Moon
Dinah Washington "The Best Of Dinah Washington"
Nat "King" Cole "The Greatest Hits"
Clairdee "Destination Moon"

Do Nothin' Till You Hear From Me
Dinah Washington "Mad About The Boy"
June Christy "Sings The Standards"
Susannah McCorkle "No More Blues"

For All We Know
Dinah Washington "Best Of Dinah-The Roulette Years"
Aretha Franklin "Jazz Moods 'Round Midnight"
June Christy "The Misty Miss Christy"

Good Morning Heartache
Dinah Washington "Smoke Gets In Your Eyes"
Lola Haag "Good Morning Heartache"
Karrin Allyson "Azure-Te"

I Didn't Know About You
Dinah Washington "Ballads"
Toni Tennille "Incurably Romantic"
Mary Stallings "Live At The Village Vangard"

I Won't Cry Anymore
Dinah Washington "The Ultimate Dinah Washington"
Marvin Gaye "Love Songs-Bedroom Ballads"
Etta James "These Foolish Things"

More Than You Know
Dinah Washington "The Legends Collection"
Jane Monheit "Never Never Land"
Stacey Kent "Close Your Eyes"

There Goes My Heart
Dinah Washington "Ballads"
Etta Jones "From The Heart"
Joni James "Platinum & Gold-The MGM Years"

There'll Be Some Changes Made
Dinah Washington "Complete On Mercury Vol. # 4"
Julie London "The Essential Julie London"
Peggy Lee "Golden Greats"

They Didn't Believe Me
Dinah Washington "The Swingin' Miss D"
Gloria Lynne "Miss Gloria Lynne"
Julie London "Julie At Home"

Without A Song
Dinah Washington "Complete On Mercury Vol. # 7"
Tierney Sutton "Dancing In The Dark"
Karen Carpenter "Carpenters-As Time Goes By"

You Go To My Head
Dinah Washington "Dinah Jams Complete Sessions"
Stacey Kent "The Collection"
Sarah Vaughan "The Best Of Sarah Vaughan"

Music notation by Forte Music / Cover design by Design Concepts